# How to Buy 1 to 3 Properties a Month

## Without Spending a Dime on Direct Mail, Putting Up Bandit Signs, or Chasing Deals in the MLS

TYLER FORD

# DEDICATION

To my wife Mimi, who always supports my crazy ideas. She is always there to help me get our homes ready to be sold so I can continue to work on generating more motivated seller leads.

To my parents, who helped me buy my first home while in college that I house-hacked to keep my expenses down. It helped me build equity so I had a nice little payday when selling the home upon graduation. And for helping me buy my first foreclosure deal that got me started down the path of real estate investing.

And lastly, to mother nature, for providing mountains to run in and trails to bike on that help me stay grounded in this universe that God has granted us.

# CONTENTS

# FOREWORD

A few years back, this guy showed up at my office door in Roseburg, Oregon, after a long trek from Tucson, Arizona. Tyler had been a real estate agent and house rehabber for over twenty-five years but was so frustrated and discouraged that he was thinking of calling it quits. Why? So many people are out there trying to get what Tyler had experienced as an entrepreneur—and he was ready to give it all up?

But I hear that story a lot. And frankly, I've experienced it myself as well. In 2012, I was at a crossroads in life and entrepreneurship myself. I had built a business that was based on what I call "boom and bust marketing," marketing that works as long as you're doing the action (cold calling, direct mail, SMS, etc.).

Think of it like a hamster wheel—you get on it, it immediately works, so you keep doing it. But eventually, you have to get off the hamster wheel because you're worn out. When you get off, the wheel slows to a stop, and you have to get back on the wheel to make it turn again. That's what most real estate agents and investors do with their marketing, and it is the primary cause of burnout and failure of agents and investors today.

On the other hand, what I did—and what Tyler did after he visited our offices in Roseburg, Oregon a few years ago—was to get off the marketing hamster wheel and start building an evergreen* marketing machine with content, credibility, and authority online. Marketing that builds momentum and actually gets better with time and creates predictability, consistency, and better ROI.

In 2012, I made the shift in my own businesses to focus on building an evergreen marketing machine and getting off the boom and bust marketing hamster wheel that led to burnout and stress. Since then, we've scaled Carrot into one of the fastest-growing companies in America, according to Inc. Magazine, and it's created the business of my dreams. One that's consistent, predictable, has momentum, and has given me true freedom and impact in my life.

Tyler took the same path after we taught him what we know, but he took it to the next level. If I were to pick the person who has executed our Carrot marketing system better than anyone else, Tyler would be toward the top of the list. He turned his business from one that was inconsistent, unpredictable, stressful—with no exciting vision for the future—into a business that he's more excited about today than ever. One that is predictable, crazy consistent, wildly profitable, and has given him back a purpose and energy in his life and business that he wondered if he'd ever have again.

If you want to learn how to get off the marketing hamster wheel as a real estate agent or investor and build a business that's predictable and builds massive momentum, this book should be at the top of your list to read this year. Tyler is one of the top online marketers in the real estate industry, and you should listen to every word he says.

—Trevor Mauch CEO Carrot.com

*Evergreen* is a term for online SEO content strategies that remain relevant and stay fresh over a long period. (More in Chapter Five.)

# INTRODUCTION

I was about ready to throw in the towel.

After nearly a quarter-century in the real estate business, I was frustrated and fed up. The market was flooded by investors spending thousands (often *many* thousands) on marketing and lead generation, and it was becoming more and more difficult to compete. Direct mail postcards, bandit signs, and chasing deals in the MLS—methods that had once generated tons of motivated seller leads—just weren't doing the trick. My cost-per-deal had risen to over two grand, and my wife and I were struggling to make ends meet.

Then I got ripped off by a trusted friend/contractor, and the wind went out of my sails.

Looking back, it was probably one of the best things that ever happened to me. I'd hired this guy (we'd been working together for a decade) to fix up a rehab home while I was out of town. I'd paid him in advance and loaded up a Home Depot card.

When I returned, nothing had been done. And I never saw him again.

I'd fallen in love with real estate in college (my first deal was a foreclosure/flip right after graduation—I broke even) and still loved it. But sometimes, it just seems that somebody's trying to tell you something. I wondered if perhaps that was the case here, and it really bummed me out.

My wife suggested (*strongly*, I might add) that I take a step back, take a break, and clear my head.

## THE EPIPHANY

I've always been an outdoor fitness guy. Biking, running, swimming, hiking—you name it. I feel like my brain just works better when my heart rate is up, almost like the increased blood flow—combined with the fresh air of the great outdoors—helps to clear out some of the junk that's accumulated in there. So, I loaded up my bike and tent, hopped into my Subaru Outback, and went to the Sierra Nevada Mountains.

There, alone beneath an almost cloudless California sky, I had my epiphany, and I followed it from the mountains to the Great Northwest, then back to Tucson, and back to the drawing board. I knew the real estate business wasn't going to revert back to the "good ol' days," There was nothing I could do to keep the "big boys" from spending their millions trying to corner the market and render us smaller investors obsolete or—if they had their way—extinct. So I made a commitment to myself, there and then, that I would formulate a plan that would enable me to get low-cost leads, lower my cost-per-deal, and bring in enough motivated sellers to do one to three deals each and every month. No more rehabs and dealing with contractors. No more Home Depot. No more spending thousands on marketing.

I wanted to fall in love with real estate again.

That was the plan.

That's what I did.

In this book, I show you how.

## WHAT THIS BOOK IS— AND WHAT IT ISN'T

Part of what I love about real estate is making people happy. Really. That may seem cheesy or disingenuous, but there really is great satisfaction in helping someone sell a property quickly to relieve some stress and put some cash in their pocket.

So, when I'm able to impart what I've learned (this book, my coaching) to help others find happiness and fulfilment—well, that really fires me up. It's the reason for this book. It's the reason I wake up every morning excited to face the day.

I'm not a real estate guru. I'm an ordinary guy who loves real estate. It's this love that has always motivated me to learn all I can about this crazy, constantly changing business, and it's this love that inspires me to share those lessons.

I'm going to show you how—with hard work, persistence, and a little patience—you can create an asset that will feed you for life. I'm going to show you—step-by-step—how to create a pipeline of motivated seller leads at a ridiculously low cost-per-lead and cost-per-deal. (I spend $300 per month to generate anywhere from ten to forty *thousand* dollars in revenue a month.) I'm going to show you a concept that will—if you put in the time and work—generate a steady flow of leads 24/7, sparking from the ember of your efforts a fire that'll continue burning for as long as you fan the flames.

Much of what you'll read may seem geeky. There's lots of information about things like *SEO*, *keywords*, *content*, *organic marketing*, and other terms that either didn't exist or had completely different meanings just a few years ago. Have no fear. I'm as far from "techy" as you can get. I'll teach it to you the same way I learned it (and which I believe is the best way to learn anything)—through practical application. By just doing it.

What I won't be teaching you in this book is how to structure a deal. Or how to sell. Or which CRM to use. Or any of the myriad of "get rich quick" schemes on which there are a ton of books already out there.

There aren't any books quite like this one. Well, I guess there is *now*.

Let's get to work!

# 1

# REALISTIC EXPECTATIONS AND THE 2-6-1 FORMULA

Check your email. Turn on your TV. Look at your social media pages. We're bombarded literally every minute of our lives by people and businesses trying to sell us something. Whether it's life insurance or home warranties or, for our purposes, real estate advice, what they're really selling you most of the time is unrealistic expectations. Every day it seems there's another book by another real estate guru with a secret method to get rich quick, usually with very little effort or investment (other than, of course, the price of the book). I sometimes wonder if there aren't more people making money *telling* people how to make money than there are people *making* money following their advice.

Fables are big business. What glitters is not always gold!

I'm not here to tell you a story. I'm here to help you create your own great story by teaching you how to build what's known in the sales world as a pipeline or deal funnel—a constant stream of motivated seller leads, also known as "the gift that keeps on giving."

You won't get rich quick following my proven methods. And there is an investment required (beyond the price of this book), but you'll mostly be investing your time and energy. The investment in dollars is such a small fraction of what others spend for the same results that it's almost laughable— although I'm sure the ones wasting their money wouldn't think so.

I've been in this business for three decades now. I've seen my share of investors lured into real estate by the promise of big paydays quickly because that was the promise they bought. Usually, within a few short months, they're gone. Just like that rehab contractor I mentioned in the introduction.

## HERE'S WHAT YOU CAN REALISTICALLY EXPECT

First of all, expect that you'll need to understand that there are no shortcuts, either in time spent working or time spent waiting. That's an absolute. Expect that I won't steer you wrong or mislead you—everything in this book is based on firsthand experience. That's how I know there aren't any shortcuts.

When things really started coming together for me, using the methods and tools I'm going to teach you, other investors and real estate pros started asking me how I did it. I happily explained what I'd been doing, but quickly found that many of those who sought advice didn't have the patience and weren't willing to put in the effort needed to make it work.

I wanted to articulate my method in a way which conveyed realistic expectations of both the time required and the eventual results, partly because I like to sum up broader concepts in concise little packages, but also because I don't dabble in mediocrity, and it's frustrating to try to help people who aren't really paying attention.

So, I came up with a formula. And it's what you can *realistically* expect.

## THE 2-6-1 FORMULA

**2**: You'll need to spend at least TWO months, working 10 to 15 hours per week, setting up the online foundation for your success: your website and its multiple elements. We'll cover these elements—including great content, SEO, domain name, an awesome "About" page, backlinks, testimonials, and more—in great detail later.

**6**: It's going to take SIX to twelve months for the search engines to work their magic. We'll explain why.

Note: I'm not saying you won't see results before six months. My first deal—using the tools and methods I'll teach you—came within sixty days. My site was ranking on the first page of the Google search results within six months. Your early results may vary, but:

**1**: This is the best number. In ONE year, you'll dominate the search engine rankings, and your pipeline will flow straight into your bank account! At this point, you can realistically expect to close one to three deals a month and bring in a six-figure yearly income. Pretty sweet. But, more importantly, you will have laid the foundation to continue getting the leads and closing the deals without investing nearly as much time or money. Currently, I spend about eight to ten hours per month maintaining my rankings and have gotten off the motivated seller lead hamster wheel. That's pretty sweet!

This formula isn't a theory. It's exactly how I did it. It's exactly how many others—through my coaching site realestatepumpkin.com—have done it.

And most important, it's exactly how YOU will do it!

# 2

# CARROT & THE EPIPHANY BRIDGE

You're going to hear me talk a lot about Carrot. In case you're not familiar with them, they're an inbound online lead generation system for real estate professionals. They're #1 in their field, and, in my opinion, set the standard for the entire industry. Just go to joincarrot.com to find out more and sign up.

For me, Carrot was kind of like my "epiphany bridge." They were the catalyst between the goals I formulated there in the Sierra Nevada Mountains and the success of my 2-6-1 Formula, making my vision of low-cost leads, a stream of motivated sellers, and doing one to three deals every month a reality.

Even prior to the "rehab rip-off" and my retreat, I'd become disillusioned with the business. I'd been racking my brain and scouring the internet, looking for ideas and inspiration to get me out of the rut, to help me compete with the big boys. I read a book called *The Pumpkin Plan* by Mike Michalowicz, in which he draws a parallel between the process for growing pumpkins and the process for growing a business: plant the right seeds, weed out the losers, and nurture the winners. Michalowicz's book was a huge motivator for me, but it was the next vegetable-themed inspiration that was really a game-changer.

## THE CARROT AT THE END OF THE TRIP

I'd heard about Carrot, checked out their website, and liked what they were about. Their mission statement, *Add humanity to business and help people regain time for the things that matter*, really resonated with me, but—as I already had a website that was limping along—I figured my best bet was to try to improve upon *that* rather than just start from scratch. That even a wounded "bird in the hand beats two in the bush."

Then I listened to one of Carrot's podcasts - or CarrotCasts, as they're called—and it moved me. Seriously. I listened to Trevor Mauch, the founder of Carrot and the podcast host, and he was so in-tune to my own way of thinking—and also, like me, seemed to truly love this business—that I knew I had to meet him and get to know more about Carrot.

So, I extended my road trip.

I got in touch with Trevor, told him that I was going to be doing an XTERRA triathlon in Tahoe City, and asked if he minded if I "drop by" (it was actually a 450-mile trip) their offices in Roseburg, Oregon after that. He said their door was open.

**My campsite on the Umpqua River east of Carrot HQ**

The entire trip itself was awesome—I checked out Bend, Oregon, and did a couple of awesome road bike rides, then headed to Roseburg.

I camped on the Umpqua River about fifteen miles east of Roseburg and Carrot HQ. I was in awe of the beauty of the Great Northwest, but it was those few hours hanging out with Trevor and his team at Carrot that forever changed my life.

I mentioned earlier that I don't really like to use the word "guru." It's overused, mainly for the purposes of selling unrealistic expectations. I will say, however, that Trevor is at least guru-*ish*. He'll probably give me a hard time for saying that next time I'm on one of his CarrotCasts or at Carrot Camp (and I've been on a few of the former and to one of the latter), but I'm serious—this guy knows more about online real estate lead generation than probably any person on the planet.

**Me and Trevor Mauch at Carrot HQ**

Yes, I *am* a Carrot affiliate (joincarrot.com, in case you forgot), meaning I'm compensated a little bit when I send folks their way. Would I be saying all these nice things about them if not for that? ABSOLUTELY! I've made much more through integrating their system with my own than they could ever pay me.

There are other options out there, and I won't tell you that you can't apply my 2-6-1 Formula using other website platforms and tools. I'm simply telling you that—if not for Carrot—I seriously doubt we'd be having this chat. I kind of doubt I'd still be in this business.

Yet here I am, hoping to help you make your own epiphany.

I will teach you more about some of the other tools and resources Carrot has to offer throughout the book. And if you need more in-depth, one-on-one coaching, I'll personally walk you through every step of my 2-6-1 Formula with your realestatepumpkin.com membership. But now I know you can't wait to get into SEO.

LET'S DO IT!

# 3

# THE POWER OF
# ORGANIC SEO

*(And Why Every Real Estate Investor Needs to
Learn How to Harness It)*

I have a confession to make… I absolutely *love* organic SEO. It's like a very fun game, and I have a blast digging into my *Carrot SEO Bible* (you can get your free download at seoforinvestors.com), making a few tweaks here and there to my sites, and scheduling Carrot content (or creating my own). I can then check my analytics (how you track the number of visitors to your site and where my sites rank on Google) to see whether

I won or lost. Using the tools I'm now teaching you, I almost always win, which means my work rarely does *not* index on Google.

I know that all sounds incredibly geeky and complicated. It may be a little geeky, but it's really not complicated. And don't forget, you can go very in-depth with all the materials in this book (I'll walk you through it step-by-step) with a membership to my coaching site at realestatepumpkin.com.

## WHAT'S ORGANIC SEO, AND WHY ARE YOU TELLING US ABOUT IT NOW?

Very good question! Let's start with "organic." In the online world, it means something totally different than that little "something" that made your Grandmother's green beans so delicious.

When you do a search—on Google, Bing, or any other search engine—the results you get will be one of two types: *paid* (at the top of each page, conveniently marked "ad") or *organic*, which are chosen by the search engine based upon what you typed into the search bar.

So, "organic" just means "free." It's kind of like Grandma's home-grown green beans, and just as awesome.

SEO is short for search engine optimization. The dictionary defines it as "the process of maximizing the number of visitors to a particular website by ensuring that the site appears high on the list of results returned by a search engine."

I like to think of SEO as a really cool income-producing exercise, or as I mentioned, a game. It's like a puzzle that pays. You're essentially trying to anticipate which words (or phrases) people will type into their phone or computer when they're trying desperately to find someone to sell their home to, and to create well-written and organized content to match their search phrases.

Those words are key. In fact, they're called "keywords." We'll talk more about those in the context of various elements of your site as we progress.

You may be wondering why I'm telling you about all this now before we've talked about such integral elements of your online presence as your domain name, your great About page, and your other killer content.

The reason is simple:

## ORGANIC SEO IS EVERYTHING!

You can have the coolest Carrot website with the greatest content in the world, but unless you're near the top of that Google or Bing search when a motivated seller wants to find you, nobody's going to pay you a visit. Sure, you can pay to get your link out there, but then it's not organic. And that's the cornerstone of the 2-6-1 Formula.

All that you do with your site—pre-launch and post-launch—should be done with SEO in mind.

I highly recommend you get your *Carrot SEO Keyword Bible for Real Estate Investors*. They've done the research and compiled a list of the keywords that bring in 80% of the leads top investors get today. You can get your free download at carrot.com/resources. You'll find lots of other resources on that page as well, including their 90-Day Action Plan, which I also highly recommend. Using both of these tools in conjunction with this 2-6-1 Formula will get you out of the starting gate more quickly and make for a smoother ride.

## THE WONDERFUL POWER OF FREE

According to Hubspot's 2020 State of Inbound Report, *Organic inbound results create 54% more leads than paid ads and save businesses $20K per year on average compared to paid marketing.* One of the main reasons for this, I believe, is that people just don't like ads. I've not seen the research to back this up, but I know that I almost always scroll past the ads when I'm doing an online search. I think we've been so bombarded by marketing over the last few generations that

we've developed an inherent distaste for ads. Again, that's just my theory, but I'm sticking to it.

What's not a theory is that organic SEO is where it's at. You do something well once and get paid over and over again. This is true for almost all types of businesses, but especially so for Real Estate investors targeting sellers who want to sell their homes quickly and without a realtor. Our bread and butter.

Now, let's put this organic SEO to work!

Grab your (orange) Bible. Haven't got it yet? Just go to seoforinvestors.com for your free download.

# 4

# WHAT'S IN A NAME? EVERYTHING!

### *Picking the Right Domain Name for City-Specific SEO Domination*

B efore we go further, I'll address a question many of you are asking right now:

*How do I build a website?*
*I know NOTHING about this stuff!*

I really didn't either, but with Carrot, you can literally have a site up in minutes with no more computer skills than are needed to order a pizza online. Seriously. Just go to joincarrot.com.

Of course, having a site up and having an awesome, money-making site are two completely different animals. One of the steps you'll take during the set-up of your Carrot site is choosing your domain name (also known as your URL, web address, or link).

I can't overemphasize the importance of your domain name to your organic SEO success! Probably one of the most common mistakes I see made by real estate investors is that their domain doesn't contain any keywords—or not the right keywords. Often, they'll let their ego get the better of them and make their own name part of their domain name. Unless you expect to get leads from people who already know about you and are looking specifically for you, resist this temptation.

## LOCATION, LOCATION, LOCATION

There is no industry I can think of for which that adage is more applicable than real estate. This is why it's vital to include the name of your city in your domain name.

Let's do a quick exercise to demonstrate. I want you to copy and paste the following into your search engine bar: Sell Tucson home fast.

What do you see? Right. A few ads. Most people scroll past those, remember? What do you see then? As you'll recall, this is where the organic search engine results begin. You should see selltucsonhomefast.com. Guess which part of that domain is a keyword?

If you answered, "all of it," you win! "Sell" is a keyword. "Tucson" is a keyword. So are "home" and "fast." These are all words someone looking to sell their Tucson home quickly would probably type into their search bar. That's my site, of course. It's the one that, as I mentioned in Chapter Two, was on the first page of several keyword searches within two weeks.

In fact, several of those top results are mine. I'll tell you all about that when we discuss the power of having multiple sites.

Besides the name of the market you're in, you'll want to consider the following when choosing your domain name:

- Unique, accurate, and memorable

  If you're hoping they'll figure out what you're all about *after* they visit your site, guess again. They won't click in the first place.
- Easy to spell and type

  The golden rule of SEO is making the experience user-friendly. Don't confuse people. And please keep in mind that just because it sounds good it doesn't mean it reads well. If you own a business called IT Scrap, you might want to think of something besides itscrap.com for your domain name.
- It stands out from the competition

  Do a little research of the local market. See what URLs they're using. Be unique. Don't try to trick people to your site by making just a tiny change to a competitor's well-known URL. That's just annoying.

Here's another question you may be asking: *What if I already have a website that I've had for years?*

If your website is ranking well on Google—awesome! We're going to show you how to capitalize on that. Your new Carrot site will be yet another lead-generating weapon in your arsenal. Again, we'll cover the power of multiple sites later.

If your site isn't ranking well, or otherwise doing what it should be doing (bringing you a steady stream of motivated sellers), consider moving your URL and site to Carrot. They'll make it easy, and their sites are optimized specifically for real estate investors. That's why they're The #1 Inbound Online Lead Generation System For Serious Real Estate Professionals.

Go to joincarrot.com, in case you haven't already been. And don't forget—I can personally walk you through every step of my 2-6-1

Formula with a membership to my coaching site—
realestatepumpkin.com.

Once your website is up and you've chosen your
domain, the real fun begins. Let's talk about creating
content.

# 5

# HOW TO CREATE CONTENT THAT WILL FEED YOU FOR LIFE

Hopefully, by now, you have your Carrot site (JoinCarrot.com if you haven't), picked out your SEO-friendly domain, and are ready to get to the "meat-and-potatoes" part of the 2-6-1 Formula—creating awesome content. If you're initially just giving this book a once-through, kind of getting your bearings before diving in, that's understandable. However, I would strongly suggest that you play (and work) along as we go. It makes the journey, not just more exciting and motivating, but more productive, too!

## WHY IS HIGH-QUALITY CONTENT IMPORTANT?

Think of the 2-6-1 Formula as a jigsaw puzzle. If you've ever put together one of these things (or watched your grandmother do it), you'll know that the best way to begin is with the outer edges. You need to create the framework. That's what you've done with your Carrot site and SEO-friendly domain. Of course, if you just leave the puzzle like that, you may get some people to take a look, but they're not going to be very impressed.

Content is the beautiful and compelling landscape you piece together within the frame of your puzzle. It's the meat and most of the potatoes. It plays, not only a vital role in getting motivated sellers to your site, but in keeping them there. And most important, it gets them to take action.

How? High-quality content helps you dominate the entire first page of search results. While your

SEO-friendly domain—as we mentioned in the previous chapter—plays a large part in this, it's the combination of these elements that will put you over the top and on your way to consistently closing one to three deals per month.

Search engines use the content on your website to determine if what you have to offer is relevant to the searcher. If I want to buy homes in Tucson, my site had better have content about *selling* homes in Tucson. That's what my future customers will be typing into the search bar.

The time and effort you put into creating killer, SEO-driven content is, in all likelihood, time and effort your competition is not putting into it. That's huge.

"But I'm not a writer."

You know what? Most of us aren't. You know who has great writers to generate SEO-friendly, real estate-specific content that can be easily customized to your market? That's right, Carrot! With Carrot's content and my diligence, I'm able to rule the first page of search engine results in my market. And I spend all of eight to ten hours per month keeping it that way—even with five websites! Once again, we'll cover the magic of multiple sites soon.

SEO experts tell us that the two most important factors in search rankings are high-quality content and link-building. We'll talk about the latter later, but first, let's discuss your site's must-have pages and the things you need to do to make them perform like rock stars.

(A note about evergreen: With very few exceptions, you'll want your content to be what's known as "evergreen." In the digital world, this refers to content without an expiration date—information that is relevant yesterday, today, and tomorrow. Always keep "evergreen" in mind when creating content. Maybe get one of those Christmas tree-shaped air fresheners to remind you!)

## ABOUT PAGE

You've heard the old adage, "You only have one chance to make a great first impression." The About page is your opportunity to do just that. It's not only your digital persona and introduction to what you and your business are about, but it's also your chance to give motivated sellers a sense of who you are and why they should trust you. (More on this in the next chapter.)

Your About page will be one of your site's most-visited pages, so be honest. Be informative. Be interesting and memorable. And—keeping in mind that search engines will mine this page to determine whether your business matches the search queries—use critical keywords like locations and real estate terms to establish yourself. Consult your Carrot SEO Bible (seoforinvestors.com).

Besides a clear picture of my smiling face, here's what you'll find on the About page of my selltucson-homefast.com site (with a few parenthetical notes along the way):

**My name is Tyler Ford. Since 1995 – when I started *Sell Tucson Home Fast*, a local real estate home-buying company – we've been helping people sell their**

**Tucson property quickly.** (Who I am, what I do, where and when I started doing it. Lots of keywords)

**As a lifelong Arizonian (I grew up here in Tucson and graduated from Northern Arizona University in Flagstaff), I love all that Tucson has to offer - and so do my wife and family!** (More personal, establishes trust)

**For over a quarter century, we've been helping people buy, sell, and finance real estate. And while I *am* a licensed Arizona real estate agent, at *Sell Tucson Home Fast* our goal is not to LIST but to *BUY* your house. We buy properties all over Arizona, but primarily in the Tucson market.** (More information and trust-establishing, more keywords)

**Selling a home can typically take several weeks to several *months* – or even LONGER. With Sell Tucson Home Fast, you can avoid the stress and hassle of a long wait!** (How we can help, why you should choose us. More keywords)

Take some time crafting your About page. Find an English-major friend or family member to help you out if needed. Keep it short and personable. ***And pay attention to keywords!***

## BLOG ARTICLES

A big factor in search engine results is relevance— to this end, it's not just keywords, but the dates those keywords were posted. Frequently updated, keyword-rich posts, especially in concert with the wealth of static keywords on your site (your domain, About page, etc.), can play a huge role in your SEO success.

Let's take another look at my **Sell Tucson Home Fast** site. The keywords in my domain, plus those on my About page, will most likely land me consistently on that first page of search results. But if I post a blog article on selling your home in Tucson, I'm going to be golden. It's like a one-two punch. Each new SEO-friendly article I post will add to my relevance in the search simply because it's new.

I'm reading your mind: You're thinking, *That's a lot of writing!* Again, that's where Carrot comes in. Carrot Content Pro members have access to twelve pre-written blog posts per month—that's about three per week! With just a little creative editing (adding your location-specific keywords, creating those internal and external backlinks we'll discuss later, having locally-relevant images, making sure post SEO settings are filled out correctly, and assigning your content city-specific tags and categories), you can have an entire month's worth of real estate-specific content scheduled to automatically post on your blog page. Go to JoinCarrot.com to find out more.

## LOCATION-SPECIFIC PAGES

You can also get great SEO results from adding location-specific pages to your site. For example, I have a page on my site dedicated to Benson, AZ—a suburb of Tucson. Simply by adding specificity—a market-within-a-market, if you will—I consistently win 60% of the first page results for relevant posts about Benson. Who can beat that? (Hint: *nobody*.)

## OTHER WAYS TO MAKE YOUR PAGES POP

You've heard that the devil is in the details. Guess what? So is the money! The care you take in creating your content is what will set you above the competition, both figuratively and—in the case of the search engine pages—literally.

Here are a few ways to get you there:

### Longtail Keyword-based Content

Simple keywords—the words or short phrases people use to search online—are often very competitive. As

I'm sure you can guess, a search for "sell my home" will yield millions upon millions of results—the first hundred or so pages populated by huge companies with huge marketing budgets. I can't compete with that. Nor can you.

Fortunately for us, people tend to be more specific in their searches—and the more specific they get, the longer the search phrase. In fact, according to WordStream. 50% of search queries are four words or longer. These are known as longtail keyword searches and provide hidden gems that can attract high-quality leads.

With the SEO tools from Carrot and a little search engine research, you can discover and rank for these keywords quickly—and dominate them!

To discover these longtail keywords, play around with your search engine. Begin typing in a phrase like "sell Tucson home," and see what the search engine suggests. For this example, you may see suggestions like "*sell Tucson home fast,*" (I like that one), "*sell Tucson home without realtor,*" or even "*sell Tucson home subject to existing mortgage.*" As you type in more words, different suggestions pop up. Make a list of those relevant suggestions and integrate them into your content. And don't just use Google or Bing (or whatever your primary search engine may be). WordStream, Moz, and SEMRush have keyword search tools that can expand your longtail keyword horizons significantly. Honestly, this stuff is fun for me as I mentioned that earlier.

### Relevant Images

Of course, search engines don't look for only words and phrases—they're also seeking out rich multimedia content, like images and videos. Use carefully selected stock photos to populate your home page and blog posts. For example, if your market is a beach town, pick photos that reflect beach living; if residents in the area are mostly retired, show images of older people. (Just not naked.)

A picture paints a thousand words. Pictures also paint quite a few *keywords*. Use relevant images, and the search engines will reward you.

## Tag, You're It!

Another crucial part of your SEO game plan is tagging your content using appropriate keywords. If your blog post is about "nightlife in Tucson," the keywords you tag it with need to reflect that. Carrot's built-in SEO tools can help, with real estate-specific tags and the option of creating your own, but there are other ways you can enhance your search engine relevance as well.

One of the most effective of these is to name and tag your images. Most people are pretty good about tagging their pages and posts with keywords. I've found, though, that I can boost my ranking a ton by taking the often-neglected step of naming and tagging the pictures.

People tend to upload images to their site with names like "IMG113.jpeg." By taking the time to rename the file with a description, you boost your site's search engine stock!

Even more often overlooked are what are known as alt tags (or alt attribute or image tags). These provide more information for search engines to help visually impaired people understand what's on your site. Search engines value machine-readable information. Alt tags that provide succinct sentences describing the image will help your rankings immensely. Include location data and target keywords to help ensure that you show up in area-specific searches.

Say your post shows an image of a family in front of their new home. An alt tag might read: "Happy family standing in front of their new home in Tucson" (Note the inclusion of the longtail keyword "new home in Tucson").

Remember that user experience is key, and that includes *all* users. You may have to alt tag a hundred of photos before you close a deal with a vision-impaired seller, but that deal can be worth thousands!

There are also tags and categories that are longtail URLs. These index really well in the search results and can add even more traffic (and motivated seller leads) to your website. This gets a little more complex than can be detailed in this book but is one of those elements I'll be walking you through with a membership to my coaching site—realestatepumpkin.com.

## YOUR KILLER CONTENT TOOLBOX

Here's a peek into my expert toolbox for total SEO domination:

1. A website with SEO support and blogging software (You know who's got that covered? Exactly. JoinCarrot.com).
2. Image editing software like Canva or PicMonkey
3. Stock photo sites like Shutterstock
4. Keyword research sites like WordStream, Moz, or SEMRush

5. In-depth coaching through realestatepumpkin.com

Congratulations—you've just filled out a big piece of the puzzle! Hopefully, you're starting to see the bigger picture, and it's starting to look beautiful.

Let's put some more pieces together, shall we?

# YOU GET MORE LEADS WHEN YOU MAKE MORE CONTENT

## TYLER FORD

www.realestatepumpkin.com

# 6

# CREDIBILITY IS KEY

Whew! We've covered a lot of ground, and you've done some important work—but we've still got plenty of ground to cover and work to do.

In this chapter, we're going to take a little break from SEO (although ideally, it'll become second nature to always be thinking about its awesome power—at least whenever you're working on your site) to talk about your credibility. As you may have guessed from the title of this chapter, it's key!

Credibility is the extent to which you're believed. If you don't have it, all the SEO and keywords in the world won't help you get it (although high search engine rankings are themselves a form of credibility, they're just the icing on the cake). It's not just the way in which you conduct your business and your life; it's how you communicate that to motivated sellers. And it's not something you can buy; it has to be earned.

In short, you want the service and value you provide to be *IN*credible, but not *UN*credible. I'm here to help you with that.

## MORE ABOUT THAT ABOUT PAGE

In the last chapter, we went over a lot of the "how" of this all-important page on your website, but only briefly touched on the "why." Why are you more qualified and trustworthy than that investor (hopefully) below you in the search engine results?

I'm always amazed by how often investors will neglect their About page and how rarely business owners of all stripes will fail to approach their website from the perspective of their potential customers. People want to know who they're doing business with, and this is probably truer for real estate than for most other fields. Selling a home is a huge deal, and your credibility will be a key factor in their decision-making.

It's more than just well-established theory—it's a fact that your About page will be the second-most visited page on your site after the home page. I look at the analytics for my various sites every day, and those numbers don't lie.

## WHY "LOCAL" IS SO MUCH MORE THAN A KEYWORD

It probably goes back to the caveman days. People just have a tendency to trust those from their own community more than out-of-towners. By the time a motivated seller reads my About page, they will have no doubt about my love of and commitment to Tucson. I mention it six times! Yes, it's very SEO-friendly to do that, but it also establishes— then reinforces—my connection to the community.

What if you don't live in your target market? Well, most likely you've been there. Talk about the things you love about it, about how much you always look forward to your visits. Honestly, it won't hurt if you almost sound apologetic that you don't live there. Just don't be fake about it.

## TESTIMONIALS/REVIEWS—THE INCREDIBLE CREDIBILITY TOOL

Even in today's digital age, with all of its technological advances and marketing tools (like the ones you're learning now), word-of-mouth always has been—and always will be—the best advertising there is. And that's what testimonials and reviews are. I think this goes back to the caveman days as well—although then testimonials were painted instead of posted and were on a much rockier platform.

But think about it (again, looking at your site from your motivated seller's point-of-view). What factors do you consider when making a major decision or purchase? We instinctively want to know what others have to say about it. It's the basic human nature.

I'm going to level with you: I didn't pay as much attention to testimonials and reviews as I should have when I launched my first Carrot site (JoinCarrot.com). But then, Carrot founder, Trevor Mauch, and I had a chat on one of his CarrotCasts (the popular podcast I mentioned earlier), and he threw out a challenge to me concerning credibility, testimonials, reviews, and citations, which we'll discuss below. I took that challenge and went to work specifically on those areas, beginning with my webuyhomesintucson.com site.

Those efforts have paid off like crazy! I can't tell you how many times I've been told, "Listen, there are a lot of people out there, but we're going with you because of your reviews." Seriously. Time and time again. I'm not exaggerating in the slightest when I say that testimonials and reviews have made me thousands!

## Citations

If it's a good review or testimonial, then there are no bad ways to use them, except to not use them. But that doesn't mean they're all created equal.

If your happy customer sends you an awesome comment via mail or through your site's Comment link or Contact page, that's great—post them on your site immediately. The best testimonials and reviews, though, are going to be through another site, such as Google, Facebook, the Better Business Bureau, or even Cash Home Buyers Directory (cashhomebuyersdirectory.com). And that's where citations come in.

Technically, any time your business or website is mentioned on another website it's a citation. Obviously, those websites I mentioned will be much more effective than having your name dropped on your niece's blog. Google and Facebook are, of course, the best places to be reviewed, and they're free. And it's always nice to have glowing reviews on the BBB website. Additionally, each citation can be built upon. When you get a glowing review on any of these sites, comment on it using your business name and website. Your comments themselves then become citations!

## HOW I GET GREAT TESTIMONIALS (WITH CITATIONS) 100% OF THE TIME

Going back to my chat with Trevor on the CarrotCast, when he challenged me to up my game regarding credibility, reviews, testimonials, and citations, I put his great suggestions to use—but also took it up a notch. After every single transaction—knowing that I've provided value and made my motivated seller's life less stressful—I send the seller an email. Of course, I thank them and tell them how much I enjoyed working with them. Then I tell them that, if they feel we exceeded their expectations (and we always do), we'd really appreciate a review. And I include the links to Google and the BBB. Then I sweeten the deal. I tell them that if they do leave a review on one (or both) of those sites, I'm going to send them a $50 Visa gift card.

It works every single time. I then give them an opportunity to make even more with a referral. I tell them that if they know somebody who needs to sell a property quick and with as little stress as possible, to have them give me a call. If we do a deal, they'll get a $500 referral fee!

## YET ANOTHER CREDIBILITY BOOST

You can never have too much credibility. Once my great About page and awesome reviews get motivated sellers to my door (or phone or inbox), I either send or hand them personally what I call my Credibility Packet. It includes even more information about how we help motivated sellers save time and avoid stress.

As part of the comprehensive, one-on-one training you'll get with a membership to my coaching site (realestatepumpkin.com), you'll get not just copies of these Credibility Packets, but also a copy of the exact email I send to my satisfied customers and which never fails to get outstanding reviews and citations, boosting not just my SEO but my credibility.

## *AND FINALLY...*

This may seem like a no-brainer, but I'm going to say it anyway: ANSWER YOUR PHONE! The more steps and technology—voicemail, email, etc.—you put between you and your motivated seller, the more likely you are to lose the deal. It's that simple. There are literally people who—if their call goes to voicemail—will simply mark you off their list and move on. Is it worth the risk just to possibly dodge a telemarketer? (That's a rhetorical question.) It's not.

So, answer your phone. That also enhances your credibility. The quicker you go from online to offline, the higher your credibility bar goes up, and the better your chances of beating out the competition.

Credibility is key!

# 7

# THE MAGIC OF
# MULTIPLE SITES

I know what you're thinking: *I'm just wrapping my head around all I need to do to get ONE site up and producing. I'm not sure I've got the time and/or money to do multiple sites!*

Well, you do. And you should. In this chapter, I'm going to tell you why. If it makes you feel any better, this is one of the few chapters where I'm going to recommend you don't actually follow along at home. You'll want to have your first site up and running and on the first page of those search engine results before you take on this facet of the 2-6-1 Formula with multiple sites. The experience and knowledge you gain there will make adding additional sites infinitely less frustrating and time-consuming.

## PLAYING THE NUMBERS GAME

The numbers don't lie. They don't even fib a little. Multiple studies done on the relationship between search engine results and CTRs (click-through rates) all say the same thing: Your chances of a motivated seller visiting your site decrease exponentially as your search engine ranking drops down the first page.

Simply put, the top organic result is going to get about a third of the clicks. The top three are going to get about two-thirds or more of the clicks. And the second page of the search engine results? You've got a better chance of getting leads by hiring a clown to stand at an intersection waving a "We Buy Homes" sign. Less than one percent of internet searches ever even make it to the second page.

Obviously—and as we've covered in previous chapters—your goal is to get that #1 spot. But what if you get the top three spots? How about the top five? I think you see where I'm going with this.

## OTHER BENEFITS OF MULTIPLE SITES

Wrapped within the numbers are some added perks to dominating the search engine results:

### The Friendliest Competition is with Yourself

Having multiple related sites increases the likelihood that your content will be found. If a particular keyword or phrase doesn't find one of your sites, it'll find another one. Larger companies do this kind of thing all the time: When Zillow acquired Trulia in 2015, they kept the Trulia.com domain. Why? Because some folks didn't get the memo. It's been five years, and Zillow still has Trulia.com. Because they're still getting results.

It's not unusual at all for me to get multiple requests from the same seller—all because I have multiple sites (each with its own unique branding) on the first pages of various search engines. This is the best indicator of a truly motivated seller there is and can only happen with high-SEO-ranking multiple sites!

## Expand Your Presence, Expand Your Reach

Say you're just starting out as an investor in one primary market—you're going to want to load that site up with the name of your market (as we talked about earlier) and optimize your online presence for that location. But what if you want to expand beyond your primary market? By having multiple sites, you can broaden your focus from local to regional and beyond.

## Fill the Niches

Wherever there's a market, there's a niche. Multiple sites can help you fill them.

Are you—like me—also a licensed real estate agent? A secondary website devoted to residential real estate can help you capture this niche and, at the same time, diversify your business and provide greater value to homeowners. If done correctly, you can even get both sites to rank for some of the same keywords. This is also a great strategy for backlinks, which we'll discuss in the next chapter.

What about mobile homes? Before you scoff, let me tell you that I was hesitant about that particular niche market; I just wasn't sure if the profit margin was worth the effort. Trust me, it is. That's why one of my sites is selltucsonmobilehomefast.com!

## IS IT REALLY WORTH THE TIME AND MONEY?

Yes. Or we wouldn't be having this chat.

Seriously, I have five Carrot sites—they cost me a whopping $150 per month. On average—once I invested the time in getting them ready for success—I spend eight to ten hours *per month* keeping them up-to-date and bringing in motivated sellers. Compared to direct mail, putting up bandit signs, or chasing deals in the MLS, it's a bargain.

And let me reiterate: We're in a business where a single deal can bring in thousands. Do we really need to be sweating the nickels and dimes? No, you don't. Not when those nickels and dimes multiply like drunken rabbits.

Of course, if not for Carrot (JoinCarrot.com), I'd be spending a lot more hours creating great content and making all of the SEO-friendly updates needed to keep crushing the search engine results. Carrot does much of that for me. The content they provide requires just a bit of customizing and location-optimizing, and their platform makes the updating a breeze. Would it be worth the time and money even if I didn't have the awesome Carrot team behind me? Yes, it would. I just wouldn't have as much time to make more money. Or sleep.

There are lots of variables and SEO strategies (like that "unique branding" mentioned above) to consider with multiple sites that are beyond the scope of this book. They're not, however, beyond the scope of my coaching membership site. Go to realestatepumpkin.com to find out more.

# 8

# BACKLINKS—THE "SECRET SAUCE" INGREDIENT

When you think about it, there are many facets of building and growing your real estate investment business with a powerful online presence—concepts like *credibility* and tools like *testimonials and reviews* that are timeless.

Backlinks, no matter how technical and daunting the word may seem, is another of those facets. Think back to your school days, when the new or unpopular kids would try to boost their social standing by befriending members of the "in" crowd, hoping their popularity would rub off.

Welcome to backlinks.

Search engines—like your old classmates—want to know that your site is relevant and respected. Backlinks (any time your site's URL is featured on another website) are how they know.

Backlinks are crucial to dominating search engine rankings but can be hard to come by. We can't control what other sites post, much in the way that we can't control who the captain of the football team hangs out with. There are resources that will promise backlinks for a price, but you don't want those. Google's pretty smart these days and can tell the legitimately acquired backlinks from those provided by a service that sticks your URL on a page about David Bowie, which can hurt your SEO rankings (and yes, there are sites which actually do that kind of thing).

Let's have a look at some of the methods I've used in concert with the other components of my 2-6-1

Formula to help build a steady stream of motivated seller leads and consistently close one to three deals each and every month.

## THE CASH HOME BUYER DIRECTORY

If you only use a single resource from this chapter, and I hope that's not the case, the Cash Home Buyer Directory (believe it or not, it's cashhomebuyerdirectory.com) is the one!

It's the captain of the football team. It's one of those things, like getting your Carrot site (JoinCarrot.com) or SEO Bible (seoforinvestors.com), that you don't want to put off.

Getting backlinks from relevant real estate websites can sometimes seem impossible. It was the missing ingredient that, without which, my recipe for SEO domination wasn't nearly so tasty. That was the challenge I faced a few years ago when I partnered with a web designer and programmer to create the CHBD. I had no idea it would take on a life of its own or evolve into such an easy way to get unlimited backlinks and citations (see Chapter Six) and index in the search engines to generate even more motivated seller leads. Now, like the old song says, "We're bad; we're nationwide." All that's required is to create a listing, build some content (like an article, discussed below) within that listing, then backlink to your own site to your heart's content. A few clicks is all it takes to create backlinks that would otherwise take months of hard work, emails, and social media hustling. Really, it's a no-brainer!

The CHBD has helped me get tons of backlinks that have played a huge role in sending my sites to the top of the search results and is a major component of the 2-6-1 Formula. The best part? It's growing every day—which means even more motivated seller leads!

If you type "sell Tucson home fast" into your search bar, you'll find my CHBD site. This will give you some examples of set-up and content (note the two backlinks to selltucsonhomefast.com). If you need more specifics on using the CHBD to get results, just go to realestatepumpkin.com and sign up for my one-on-one coaching!

## OTHER WAYS TO GET BACKLINKS

Although the Cash Home Buyer Directory is the simplest, it's certainly not the only way to get those valuable backlinks. These may require a bit more time and effort, but my experience has been that—when it comes to this valuable component of the 2-6-1 Formula—it's definitely worth it!

### Articles On Other Platforms
### With Backlinks To Your Investor Site

One of the best ways to get your brand out there and get valuable backlinks is through articles outside your investor website relating to real estate investing, where you're able to either include a link to your investor website within the article or include it in the article's credits.

When I'm driving around—or any time I have a free moment—my mind is constantly thinking of new ideas that might translate into articles or other ways to get those motivated seller leads. I have a friend who's a songwriter, and he tells me that he always has his "antenna up," that ideas for songs can come from the simplest sources, such as a piece of conversation, a radio ad, a billboard, etc. It's the same with what we do. Whenever I get an idea, I make a note then spend some time trying to come up with ways to work that idea into great content—like an article, blog post, or press release. There are also times when the great content provided by Carrot will spark an idea: a way to expand or approach the subject from a different angle on another site (and, of course, with a backlink to your investor site).

Again, you don't have to be Hemingway to come up with this stuff. The key is to organize your thoughts, make notes of the bullet points, then just roll up your sleeves and write. As with your About page, you can also outsource the actual writing. There are some great freelancing websites where you can find someone to take your ideas and turn them into well-written content for really reasonable rates.

Articles and blog posts (which we covered in Chapter Five) are often be interchangeable, but, as a rule of thumb, a blog post can be as short or as long as you like, whereas an article will need to be at least five hundred words or so. If you do a search for "cash home buyer directory backlinks for real estate investors," you'll find an article I wrote on this very subject! This was, of course, posted on CHBD's website, but you can also submit articles to any website that deals with real estate investing. These sites are always hungry for original content. Just do a search for "submit real estate investing articles," and you'll get lots of ideas.

## Press Releases

Another great way to get backlinks—and one with the potential for an even wider audience—is through press releases. We usually think of a press release as a news item of interest to the general public, but almost any piece of content can be structured as a press release. For a couple of examples, go to webwire.com (a great source for submitting press releases) and search "Tucson Home Buyer." You'll see some of the press releases I've put out the past couple of years, which are another great resource for quality backlinks. Another big bonus is that these will often index on the search engines, pushing your competition down the ranks.

Press releases, which have specific release dates and are generally intended to create a sense of urgency, are one of the few exceptions to the Evergreen Rule mentioned previously. They're especially good for announcing things like launching your business or limited-time promotions. Use your imagination.

## Create Social Media Shareable Content

Whether it's Facebook, Twitter, or Instagram, social media offers an opportunity to reach a huge audience—including those valued motivated sellers—and to get those all-important backlinks. Remember, your focus should be on organic—not on those paid ads we've all come to know and hate.

The key to successful social media promotion is create content, which is brief, informative, and easily shareable. With the exception of Twitter, visual is good. One thing to definitely avoid is the temptation to spam your URL to non-relevant pages. This does you more harm than good and only hurts your credibility. Post on your own social media accounts and join as many relevant sites as you can and post on those. It also doesn't hurt at all to be an active member on those other sites. Offer comment and encouragement to others who post, and you'll find them much more likely to reciprocate.

## More Multiple-Site Magic

Another great way to use those multiple sites we discussed in the last chapter. You can cross-link blogs and landing pages from one of your sites to the others, but don't overdo it! Remember, Google is pretty smart; their algorithms can snuff out excessive backlink-stuffing and penalize you for it with lowered search engine results.

Of all the tools for enhancing SEO and getting your site (hopefully, sites) to dominate those first-page search results, backlinks—when acquired the right way—probably have the greatest potential. But remember the "6" part of the 2-6-1 Formula: *backlinks take time.*

And it's time incredibly well-spent!

# 9

# WHOLESALE BUYERS LIST HACK

*How to Build a HUGE Wholesale Buyers List*
*From Your Carrot Investor Site(s)*

This book—like the 2-6-1 Formula—is all about getting motivated sellers consistently knocking on your door. And, hopefully, you've learned a ton and have already started implementing much of it (hint: JoinCarrot.com, seoforinvestors.com, and cashhomebuyerdirectory.com).

Now, I'm going to take a short detour into generating a huge buyers list, just a couple of cool (and simple) little tricks you can do as you're building your Carrot investor site(s).

## WHEN YOU BECOME THE SELLER

There are many options for what to do once the deal is closed (or even before)—all sorts of models, from full rehabs to listing on the MLS to assignments and beyond. My model—which I'll tell you more about in the next chapter—is based on the goal of making the most amount of money in the least amount of time with the least amount of work. In some cases, that will mean wholesaling, or selling directly to a buyer, without listing in the MLS. That may seem like another no-brainer, but you'd be surprised. I've found that having my own totally organic Wholesale Buyers List—a list of investors looking to buy off-market deals to fix and flip, keep as rentals, or any non-MLS options—is a great tool to help me turn those one to three deals each and every month I've told you about into profit!

## MAKE YOUR INVESTOR SITE(S) PULL DOUBLE-DUTY

As you scroll down the home page of webuyhomesintucson.com (one of our company's sites), you'll see that it follows the guidelines of the 2-6-1 Formula. From content to keywords, it's all geared toward getting motivated sellers to reach out. However, at the bottom of the page, you'll see another navigation bar with a few more options than the navigation bar up top. One of the page links you'll see down there, tucked between Blog and Privacy Policy, is Wholesale Buyers. When you go to that page, you see content with keywords and phrases geared more toward buyers—wholesale, off-market, fix and flip—along with an opt-in form to sign up to our Wholesale Buyers List (WBL). Now Google "Tucson wholesale properties for sale." What do you see? That's right. There, among various other websites dedicated solely to attracting investors, you'll find *our* page.

Why does this matter? Two reasons. First, of course, is that it's a great way to build your WBL (wholesale buyers list). Second, you have competition at both ends of the deal, so any time one of your sites ranks on the first page of the search results for any keywords or phrases, it means one of your competitors is on the second page.

## THE HACK

I added our Tucson Wholesale Properties page after stumbling upon a little trick (or hack) regarding a location page I created, growing my WBL every single day!

First of all, this differs from the location-specific pages we covered in Chapter Five in that the location page is a type of page listed on your Carrot dashboard under "Content." This feature allows you yet another way to use your location to enhance your SEO and increase your ranking. But—as I had "Tucson" not only in my URL but sprinkled liberally throughout my content—I thought I'd try a different approach. I created a location page showing investors where the local foreclosure auctions are held. A map is automatically inserted on the page when you enter the address, so I just added some keyword-rich content and some images, along with that same opt-in for my WBL.

Now do a search for "Tucson foreclosure location." There we are! I now have a WBL with over four hundred names—and growing daily—all generated from a site that is primarily aimed at home sellers.

A Wholesale Buyers List is a great addition to your exit-strategy toolbox, but also takes some time. The sooner you start building yours, the closer you'll be to making the most amount of money in the least amount of time. And that's the name of the game!

And—as with everything in this book—I dive much deeper into creating your own huge WBL with a membership to my coaching site! Just go to realestatepumpkin.com.

# 10

## MY MODEL—WHY SETTLE FOR 100%?

Congratulations! You now know everything you've always wanted to know about the 2-6-1 Formula but didn't know to ask!

My primary goal with this book, as the title states, is to show you how to generate enough motivated seller leads to consistently close one to three deals per month. You now have all the tools; all you need is the work and the patience.

The cool thing about the 2-6-1 Formula is that it'll work regardless of your business model. Whether you want to wholesale, fix and flip, or turn your acquisitions into rentals, this plan will get you on your way. After all, without the motivated sellers, there's nothing.

Whether you're a licensed real estate agent or not, this plan will work for you!

That being said, I'm now going to tell you about my model, beginning with:

## WHY YOU ABSOLUTELY *SHOULD* BE AN INVESTOR/AGENT!

My friend and Carrot mentor, Trevor Mauch, hosted one of his popular CarrotCasts (episode #194) on the topic "Are Real Estate Investors The Underbelly of The Real Estate Industry?" As the topic suggests, he talked about this rather sad and unwarranted reputation we've gained over the years, mostly as a result of a few bad eggs—which, as Trevor points out, are to be found in every industry.

Trevor also correctly observes that—in our ability to turn properties quickly and get our customers real money real quick, without all the stresses and headaches of the traditional real estate route—we're filling a niche in the market long ignored by the traditional real estate model.

I imagine many of you are nodding your heads, wondering how this leads up to why you should be an agent. The reasons are two-fold, and both self-serving and selfless. As an investor/agent, you're simply able to help more people. And that's more profitable than a "niche."

I like helping people. I like making money. So, I *love* making more money by helping more people! And the bottom line is that the more options you're able to offer your sellers, the more deals you will close. And the more deals you close in the least amount of time, the more money you make. *That's* my "model."

Which leads me to eXp Realty, and how their model and my model mesh so beautifully and profitably!

## THE eXp REALTY MODEL

As Netflix has done for movies, as iTunes has done for music, and as Amazon has done for—well, everything—eXp has taken real estate out of the brick-and-mortar world and into the clouds. Or, rather, the Cloud. With eXp, your office is wherever you are! Add to that the training and technologies available (just their fully integrated IDX website and CRM would run you $6,000 per year!), and the opportunities they offer to make residual income through stock-awards and agent referrals, you can see why eXp Realty has experienced a 172% year-over-year growth since their inception in 2009. They've more than tripled since I signed on just two years ago!

## WHY SETTLE FOR 100%?

That sounds ambitious, doesn't it? It's not.

The reality of realty today is that it's so competitive, and there are so many able to out-spend you to get those motivated sellers and make the deals, that you have to leverage every resource available to come out on top. Becoming an investor/agent with eXp Realty is a great way to leverage a great resource!

As mentioned, you can still use what you've learned in this book to make some real money even if you're not an agent, especially once you build your Wholesale Buyers List. What you can't do is make money in your sleep! By leveraging the eXp model with my own, I'm able to do just that.

I like to hotel, which is basically buying a property, then turning around and selling it as-is in the MLS. Coupled with the large WBL I've built, I have options to sell fast for the most amount of money in the least amount of time with the least hassle. I can do that all day long and make a decent profit in a short time.

As an eXp investor/agent, I can list a property on the MLS and make a much greater profit in less time because I've got the entire MLS bidding. We'll often get several full price offers on a property within 72 hours this way!

But I'm still not making money in my sleep. That's where eXp's stock awards and agent referrals come in. As an investor/agent with eXp, I'm able to apply a portion of my commissions toward purchasing eXp stock at a discount to the market (ticker symbol EXPI), and I'm also getting a monthly revenue share payment for agents I've referred to eXp. And my revenue share commission comes out of eXp's end: "This amount is taken out of eXp's split and not from the agents."

So, by using a combination of stock awards and monthly revenue share, I'm not only making a 100% profit but a nice monthly residual income.

Because why settle for 100%?

## NOW WHAT?

Well, as Porky the Pig says at the end of those old Warner Brothers cartoons, "Th-Th-that's all folks!"

But, really, it's just the beginning. I've given you the tools, now you just have to do the work!

By following the guidelines I've laid out in this book, you can realistically expect to, within one year, generate enough motivated seller leads to close one to three deals each month. By using all the tools I've provided (listed below), you can make the absolute most of the 2-6-1 Formula!

I'd love to get your comments/reviews/success stories. Just shoot me a line at support@realestatepumpkin.com. Or, if you'd like one-on-one coaching, go to realestatepumpkin.com.

I hope to hear from you!

## THE 2-6-1 FORMULA TOOLBOX RECAP

1. Your Carrot site (JoinCarrot.com)
2. Your SEO Bible (seoforinvestors.com)
3. Your Coaching Membership (realestatepumpkin.com)
4. Your Killer Content
   - Image editing software like Canva or PicMonkey.
   - Stock Photo Sites like Shutterstock.
   - Keyword-research sites like WordStream, Moz, or SEMRush.

5. Your Backlinks Tool
   (cashhomebuyerdirectory.com)
6. Find out more about eXp Realty
   (whysettlefor100.com)

# ABOUT THE AUTHOR

Tyler Ford is a Tucson, Arizona-based real estate investor, agent, and entrepreneur. A life-long Arizonan, he caught the real estate bug while still in college at Northern Arizona State University in Flagstaff, interning during the summer in Tucson with Grubb & Ellis, a commercial real estate agency.

"I'd helped put together a few deals that first summer, but they couldn't pay me because I didn't have my license," Tyler says. "I got my license the second summer."

It was also during college that he got his first taste of homeownership and property management.

"It was a house near the college my parents helped me buy. I was able to rent one room to a classmate, build up equity, and essentially live mortgage expense-free," Tyler recalls.

Upon graduation, he wasted no time getting into real estate investment, buying his first "fix and flip" property at a local foreclosure auction.

"I put a lot of time and effort into that house," he says." At the end of the day I was able to get out of it for just break-even, but I certainly learned a lot, and that's really what got me hooked. I've been buying and selling real estate ever since."

Tyler was eventually drawn to the mortgage side of the real estate business, where he was recognized for being the nation's top-producing loan officer and leading the #1 mortgage team in the country at the Warren Buffet-owned Home Services.

"Closing over 1,500 loans required working closely with listing and selling agents and escrow companies to ensure smooth real estate transactions," says Tyler. "That experience, which gave me firsthand knowledge of how to facilitate a smooth closing, still benefits my real estate clients and real estate investment business today."

Although he remained involved in investing during his mortgage career (he began selltucsonhomesfast.com in 1995), he returned full-time to the investor/agent side of things following 2007's real estate bubble burst.

Not much more than a decade later, Tyler felt as if his *own* bubble had burst.

"It was just getting harder and harder to compete with the bigger companies flooding the market from out-of-state," he says. "They had money and resources I just couldn't match, and it was getting tough to make ends meet."

But from the ashes of despair rose salvation. And it came in the form of a Carrot.

"I said a prayer, and it was answered," Tyler says, reflecting on his soul-searching trip to the Sierra Nevada Mountains that culminated in a visit to the headquarters of the real estate website, Carrot, in Oregon. And that led to the 2-6-1 Formula.

"That trip is what turned the tide," he says, smiling. "God answers prayers."

Like Tucson in the summer, Tyler's real estate career has never been hotter. Today, he not only closes more deals faster than ever before, but he also uses his knowledge and experience to show other investors and agents how to do the same—whether through his one-on-one coaching, books (like this one), or his dedicated involvement with eXp Realty.

"If you're an investor, I can help you do it right. If you're an agent, I can help you—through the power of eXp—get much more than a commission check."

Tyler and his wife Mimi (who helps with their business) live in Tucson. When not buying or selling real estate, they're both avid cyclists, runners, and swimmers, and love the outdoors.

Made in the USA
Monee, IL
24 July 2020

36948727R00059